THE INVENTION

Where we put on our inventive-thinking caps to examine gadgets, gizmos, and contraptions.

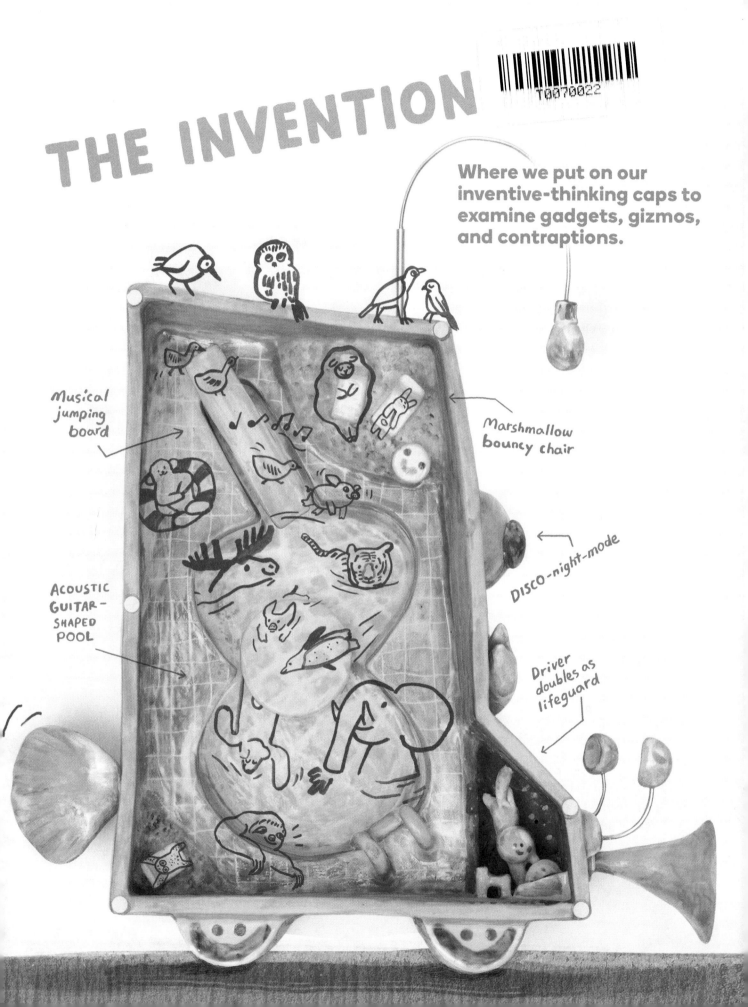

Musical jumping board

Marshmallow bouncy chair

ACOUSTIC GUITAR-SHAPED POOL

DISCO-night-mode

Driver doubles as lifeguard

FROM US TO YOU...

the invention issue

In place of the traditional LETTER FROM THE EDITOR page, we bring you a sampling from all our contributors.

OUR CONTRIBUTORS RESPOND:
WHAT PROBLEMS WOULD YOU LIKE AN INVENTION TO SOLVE? SHARE A SMALL PROBLEM AND A LARGE PROBLEM.

MUZZY
"I want jeans that automatically adjust sizes so I don't have to buy new ones if my weight changes."

YUK FUN
"We would like all avocados in the store to be perfectly ripe."

ADAM HIGTON
"Like most people, I think I spend too much time looking at screens. A pair of tiny eye curtains that close automatically when my eyes feel sleepy."

JAMYELESE RYER
"If someone loses their cell phone, how can they connect? I think a clever new kind of public phone should be available!"

JULIE BENBASSAT
"Stubbing your toe or elbow. The invention: Tiny toe and elbow shields that are stylish to wear and cushion the blow."

LAYLA FORREST-WHITE
"I am convinced that I came up with the Shazam app, or at least recognized its pressing need before it came into existence. I'm lucky that my desire to immediately know what song is playing has been satisfied."

YULIA DROBOVA
"I would like a quicker form of transportation. Like if you could close your eyes and then open them and be in the place of your choosing."

DAVID HUANG
"I'd like a language input machine so we can be fed languages faster instead of having to learn them slowly. And an emotion translator to clearly understand people better."

smaller problems:

DON'T FIT

NEW PUBLIC PHONES

ELBOW SHIELDS

TIRED EYES

PERFECTLY RIPE AVOCADOS

FASTER TRANSPORTATION

ADAM HIGTON
"In the UK our current government stands by while companies discharge raw sewage into our sea and rivers. Maybe it should be re-routed into a pipeline leading to the various companies' front doors?"

JAMYELESE RYER
"Clean all of the Earth's polluted drinking water."

DAVID HUANG
"I'd make a medical diagnosis machine to give us access to free and better healthcare at the most urgent times."

YUK FUN
"We'd like wildlife to flourish!"

larger problems:

ENOUGH HOUSING

URGENT MEDICAL CARE

UNCLEAN DRINKING WATER

POLLUTED RIVERS

TOO MUCH TRASH →

JULIE BENBASSAT
"The excess trash that goes into landfills, oceans, and other ecosystems. The invention: A machine that converts trash into soil."

LAYLA FORREST-WHITE
"I wish there were just and equitable means of exchange, where everyone's individual resources and abilities could adequately provide for their needs."

MUZZY
"I also want an invention that eliminates the need to eat. I would have so much more time and so many less worries if I didn't need to eat three times a day."

YULIA DROBOVA
"Affordable housing for everyone."

inside

iLLUSTORiA

MEET SPECIAL GUESTS

CHAPTER 1

LAUGH AND PLAY

GRAB A FRIEND & TRY THESE!

CHAPTER 2

READ AND LEARN

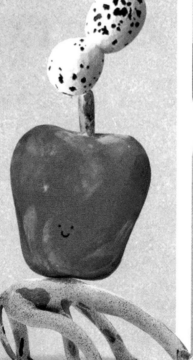

ILLUSTORIA IS THE OFFICIAL PUBLICATION OF THE INTERNATIONAL ALLIANCE OF YOUTH WRITING CENTERS

OUR CHAPTER PAGES IN THIS ISSUE FEATURE TYPOGRAPHICAL ART BY ADAM HIGTON.

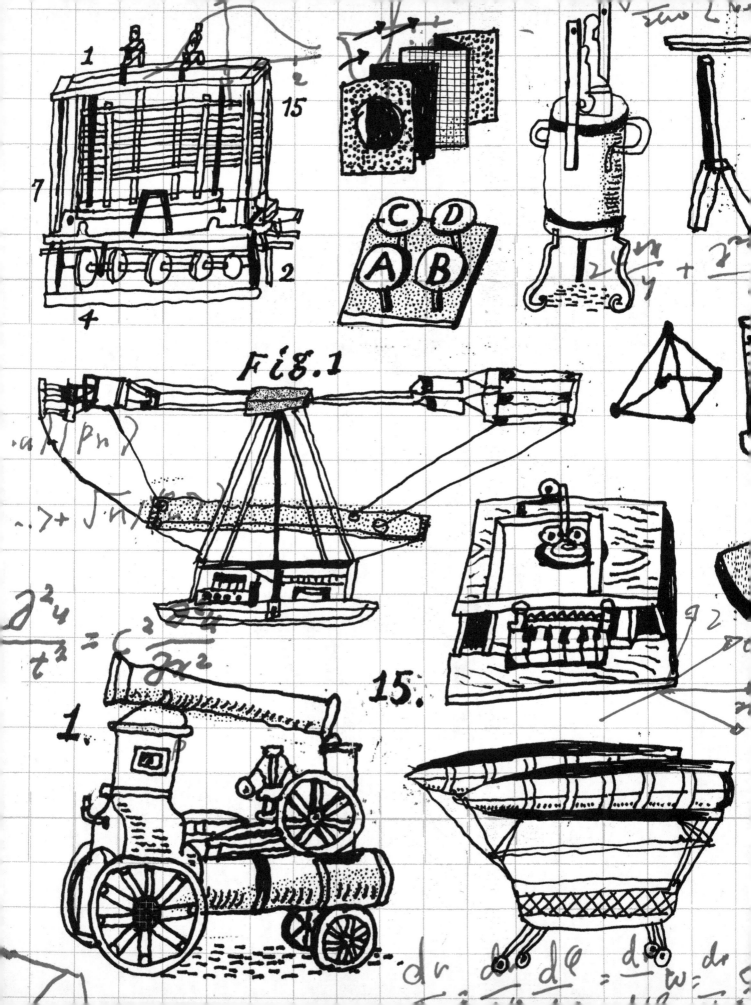

Fig.1

15.

1.

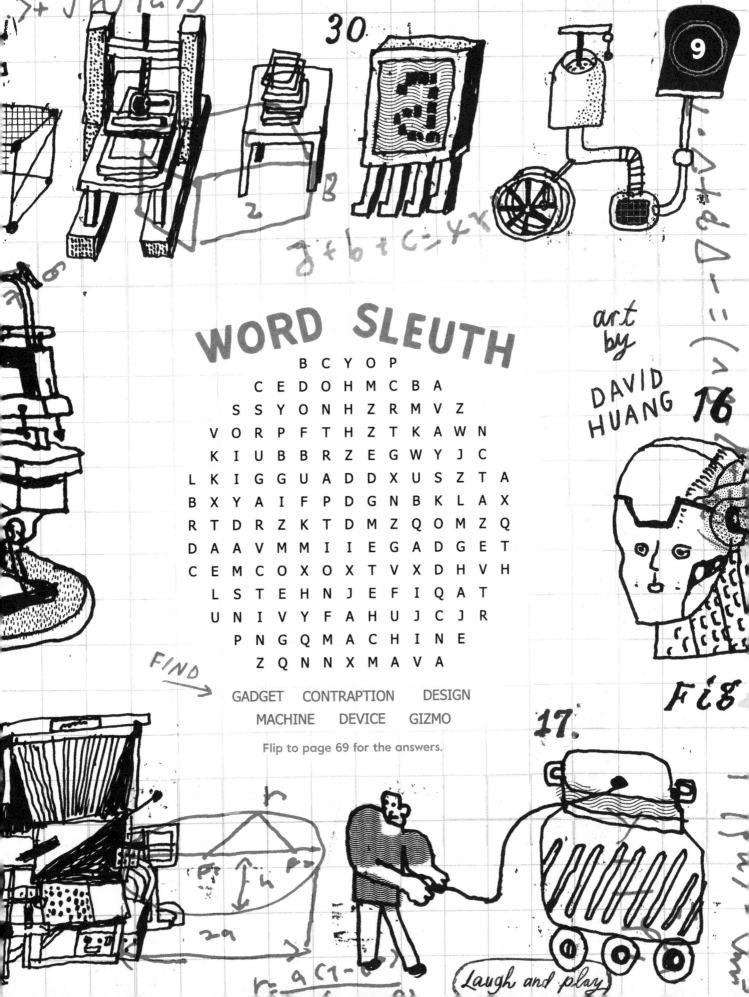

WORD SLEUTH

art by **DAVID HUANG**

```
    B C Y O P
  C E D O H M C B A
  S S Y O N H Z R M V Z
V O R P F T H Z T K A W N
K I U B B R Z E G W Y J C
L K I G G U A D D X U S Z T A
B X Y A I F P D G N B K L A X
R T D R Z K T D M Z Q O M Z Q
D A A V M M I I E G A D G E T
C E M C O X O X T V X D H V H
  L S T E H N J E F I Q A T
  U N I V Y F A H U J C J R
    P N G Q M A C H I N E
    Z Q N N X M A V A
```

FIND →

GADGET   CONTRAPTION   DESIGN
MACHINE   DEVICE   GIZMO

Flip to page 69 for the answers.

Laugh and play

SAY WHAT!?

MATCH THE SAYING TO THE IMAGE   art by AARON GONZALEZ

Lookout.
I worry that I have
bad luck today.

Tasty things taste better
when shared among friends.

Don't call me two-faced,
I just happen to like strange
fashion accessories.

I'm not sure if this sunscreen
works, my skin has never been
the shade of a grape before.

I am happy
to see you,
you're starting to really
grow on me!

Meow.
Mow mew me meowwww.

STORY STARTER CARDS

words by AMY SUMERTON

INSTRUCTIONS

Have you ever started a story thinking it would turn out one way, but then, as you wrote it, surprised yourself (and your characters!) by creating something different? Writers do this all the time; plans for a story often change as it takes shape—just one (of many!) things that makes writing such a fun and exciting activity for your brain!

STEPS

For this Story Starter exercise, you're invited to use these silly vintage photographs to create short stories that play with this idea in a more literal way. What were the creators of these goofy inventions trying to construct... and what did they actually end up inventing?

For example, using the photo on the bottom left, perhaps someone was trying to create a bike that you could ride on water, but instead ended up with a moving carnival for a band of hamsters! That became famous, and traveled the world to great fanfare and acclaim! That eventually went down in history as the Hamster Fam Band-Os, which totally overshadowed the inventor, whose name is no longer even known!

EXTRA OBSERVATION QUESTIONS

Look at each of the photos on the opposite page.
What wacky, weird thing did the inventor set out to make?
What was the surprising creation they wound up with?

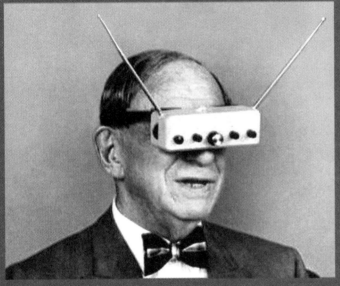

Cut out the Story Starter cards on the reverse side. ✂

Can you try to recreate any of these, using cardboard, tape, and paint?

What would your outfit look like if you dressed as an inventor for Halloween? Can you draw your idea or write about it?

How might the process of inventing be shown in comic strip format?

Interview your friends: What do they think these inventions do? Are everyone's answers different or are some similar?

Try drawing a gadget that would make anyone who looks at it automatically laugh.

BRIGHT IDE💡S

CAN YOU FIND THE TWO LIGHTBULBS THAT ARE EXACTLY THE SAME?

Did you know? Thomas Edison didn't actually invent the light bulb. His factory created them, but the pieces and parts relied on many thinkers and inventors, such as Lewis Howard Latimer, who designed improvements to the carbon filaments. Without Latimer's idea, it would have been impossible to mass produce the affordable light bulbs we rely upon so much today.

yoto

AGES 3-12+

Let kids lead the way

NO MICROPHONE, CAMERA OR ADS

Yoto Player lets kids explore hundreds of stories, albums, activities and more.

read and learn

TYPOGRAPHICAL ART BY ADAM HIGTON.

RISOGRAPH PRINTING with AARON GONZALEZ of FLOSS EDITIONS

FLOSS EDITIONS IS A RISOGRAPH PRINTING AND PUBLISHING HOUSE RUN BY MEG FRANSEE AND AARON GONZALEZ IN OAKLAND, CALIFORNIA. WE ASKED AARON A FEW QUESTIONS ABOUT HOW THEIR BUSINESS BEGAN, AND HOW THE FASCINATING MACHINE AT THE HEART OF THIS ENTERPRISE WORKS.

How did the name of your printing press come about?

When my partner and I first started our press, we were on a very aggressive flossing kick, like constantly reminding each other to floss after meals, making sure we didn't go to sleep without flossing, stuff like that. Anyways, we got to thinking about how making art is like flossing, sometimes you hate to do it and you might even bleed, but ultimately you know you should push through because it's good for your health.

What is the scope of the press? What do you currently offer, and what do you hope to offer?

Throughout our existence, we've published everything from comics, to poetry, to informational pamphlets, and whatever falls in between. We try to not be constrained by genre or a specific style and instead focus our efforts on publishing work from artists with whom we feel we share similar values and a lot of the time that ends up being our friends or folks in our immediate community. When we choose to work with someone we usually don't have a vision of what the publication will be, and we like to think of ourselves as facilitators helping artists achieve their vision. This approach has led us in some interesting directions I don't think we would have arrived at otherwise, and I'm really happy about that.

That being said, over time our publications have skewed into more labor intensive territories (for example, every perfect-bound book we made is bound by hand) which makes them a little more financially inaccessible than we like, so it's my hope that in the future we can get back to putting out more accessible publications.

Was there a moment when you felt clear about opening your own risoprint studio?
I don't think there was a specific moment, it all kind of just happened naturally and luckily for us risograph printing and publishing really started to gain popularity after we got our legs under us.

When I started to see riso publications popping up at book fairs and zine fests, I was immediately drawn to the vibrancy and texture of the prints. It somehow felt more tangible than other digital printing methods. But what really drew me to picking it up was the sheer accessibility of the medium. When I first started, I hadn't done any kind of printmaking, but the (relative) ease of use of the machines coupled with the incredibly passionate community of riso printers made it feel possible.

read and learn

Why do you think an invention from the past century has been gaining popularity?

I think it's a confluence of things that have formed a kind of a perfect storm for risograph printing to thrive. As I mentioned earlier, for artists, printers, and publishers it's a pretty accessible medium. Most of the factors that make other printing methods inaccessible are more or less removed. Risograph printers relatively inexpensive (though this has changed over time and it's much harder to find an older machine now), they don't take up a ton of space, and they're easy to use. With a riso, anyone can turn a bedroom into a capable printing press.

For consumers and appreciators, I think people are hungry for more tangible or analog forms of media. I don't think it's a coincidence that riso printed materials have gained popularity at a time when sales of vinyl records are at an all time high. I don't know what it is exactly, but maybe people are looking for a more personal connection to the content they consume and with riso you can see the humanness in the prints.

Ultimate dream project: What do you hope to do someday with the press?

Children's books! We recently became parents and have been building a library of books for our little one, and I've just been amazed at the genius of some of these publications. I love that they never take themselves too seriously because of their audience, yet they still find a way to be impactful. If we ever do move in that direction, we'd probably have to find a manufacturer for the books—which doesn't sound fun—but I don't think parents want riso ink all over their kid's hands when they're just trying to read a book.

Describe a favorite project.

My partner and I made a book called *Coolidge*. It is a collection of still-life illustrations of things around our house, named after the street we lived on at the time. We made it for ourselves as a love-letter to our first shared home, but the response to it was really positive and it was really cool to see people stoked on it. We don't live there anymore but every now and then we'll flip through it and get nostalgic for our past lives. We can't wait to share it with our son when he's older and maybe he'll want to make a book about where we live now!

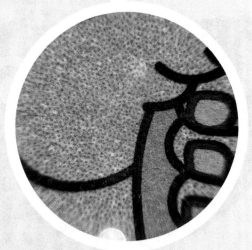

the scoop on RISO:

WHERE DOES IT COME FROM?

Risograph (pronounced "riz-OH!-graph") is a special type of printer from Japan, developed in the 1980s. The name comes from the Japanese word riso, which means "ideal." They were originally intended as printers for offices and schools because they are so fast and easy to use. These days, risograph printing has exploded in popularity as a printing option for artists around the world.

Why do artists love this bulky, gray machine? The ink choices include vivid colors (like fluorescent pink!) that other printers can't use. Inks are plant-based and inexpensive—great for printing posters and zines on a budget. Every ink color "lives" in its own portable drum, which is inserted into the machine as it is needed. This eliminates ink waste and also the need for washing stations, required by other printing methods. Especially when using recycled papers, riso printing is one of the most green and sustainable print methods around.

However, perfectionists should beware! Risographs often don't print with precision, and mistakes are easy to make. This unpredictability can be exciting for those who embrace imperfection. In this sense, each print from a risograph has tiny (or big) differences, and is therefore unique.

Three cheers for this loveable, sometimes grumpy, 80's-era machine... and its new-found fame!

HOW DOES IT WORK?

This is a risograph machine*! Risograph machines make an image by printing layers of color on top of each other, one layer at a time. To make each layer, the original image is scanned and then turned onto thousands of tiny dots using thermal heat spots that burn holes onto a master screen. This master screen is then wrapped around a print drum. The drum pushes ink through the screen and onto paper as it passes through the machine. This is why you can see tiny dots when you look really closely at a the image on the left.

*Turn to Deeper Dive on page 68 to find a risoprint center in a city near you.

This is a four color separation. Can you identify all four colors?

read and learn

CREATURE FEATURE

words by **Amy Sumerton** *art by* **Julie Benbassat**

> Greetings, humans! Doc Anthurium, here.

Doc Anthurium—scientist and, ahem, an *actual flower*—here with you again today to learn more about some animals' mysterious and inventive survival strategies!

For the arachnophobic (those with an extreme fear of spiders), the diving bell spider is truly the stuff of nightmares! Their "diving bell," which looks like a large bubble, behaves like a gill and pulls oxygen from the water. This means these clever creatures only need to hit the surface of the water once a day to supplement their air supply!

Since they're found underwater and have a painful bite—which leaves victims suffering for several days—you'll want to watch where you step when swimming in Europe and Asia.

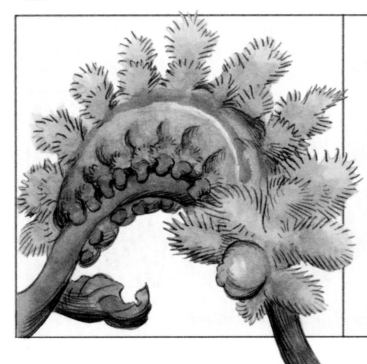

If a fear of spiders isn't your thing, how about stinging caterpillars? In their larval stage, Io moths are covered in spines... that are connected to poison glands. Come into contact with the spines, and suffer the consequences: a sensation not unlike a painful bee sting!

Beautiful and dangerous, these caterpillars grow into moths that have owl-like eyespots on their wings, making them truly terrifying to small mammals and birds. One could say they're quite sinister in all their stages; I say they've cleverly created effective ways to protect themselves.

The first time I encountered a pangolin, I could not believe my eyes! These shy mammals are covered in an armor of overlapping keratin scales!

These scales provide good defense against predators, and so does their behavior: if threatened, pangolins quickly curl into a ball to protect their undersides.

They also hiss and puff, and lash their powerful, sharp-edged tails. They need these fancy accouterments: while they have sharp claws, they have no teeth, just sticky, extremely long (up to half the length of their bodies!) tongues.

*Turn to Deeper Dive on page 68 to see photos.

Are you sitting down? You might want to, as the axolotl's survival strategy is truly astonishing! These salamanders, also known as Mexican walking fish, have the ability to regenerate organs and limbs!

In just a few weeks, an axolotl can grow back a lost limb, and they can even regenerate their lungs, hearts, spinal cords, and parts of their brains!

Even more mysteriously, scientists have discovered that they can regrow the same limb up to five times... but then they stop!

read and learn

ACCIDENTAL INVENTION BY TEEN CHEMIST CHANGES HISTORY OF FASHION

WORDS BY **JAMYELESE RYER**   ART BY **STACEY ROZICH**

HISTORICAL SETTING

Envision 1856 London, if you can, and a crowded street with everyone wearing an array of colors... except purple. Before an eighteen-year-old named William Henry Perkin accidentally messed up his chemistry lessons, purple fabric was extremely rare and costly.

HOMEWORK GONE WRONG

A science student, studying chemistry at London's Royal College of Chemistry, William had some serious homework over spring break. He was tasked with experimenting for a synthetic version of quinine, which would have been a huge medical breakthrough to help the common disease of malaria.

SURPRISING RESULT

So, he took his work home to his apartment on Cable St. and set up a work station. After many failures, William began cleaning some leftover black inky gunk with alcohol, and noticed a vibrant purple color in the beaker. Following his curiosity, William experimented more to find that the synthetic dye held fast to clothing materials. Shifting his work from medicine to the color purple absolutely revolutionized the clothing business.

REVOLUTIONARY

Why? Because until Perkin made his discovery, purple was painstakingly made from the natural world, and the very best purple that didn't fade was extracted from the little murex shell who, ironically, made the color to ward off predators. Millions of shells were taken from the sea, boiled in giant lead vats, and discarded in mountainous piles. It was so expensive, only royalty could wear it... plus, this process made a terrible stink! Perkin called his purple dye "mauveine" and it became a popular color that people could finally afford to wear. (Are you wearing purple right now?)

OTHER YOUNG INVENTORS

There have been many other inventions of renown crafted by young people, such as:

The trampoline
Earmuffs
Christmas tree lights
Braille
Swimming flippers
And... Popsicles!
Just to name a few.

Visit our Deeper Dive section on page 68 for more books and resources on the subject of young inventors.

WE ASKED A POET...

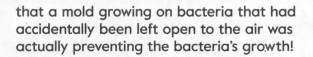

DR. LAYLA FORREST-WHITE IS A POET LIVING IN THE BAY AREA. WE GAVE HER AN ARTICLE TO READ ABOUT THE HISTORY OF ACCIDENTAL INVENTIONS. HERE ARE HER THOUGHTS.

Did you know that sometimes lurking, sometimes weaving inside our words are other words and other languages? French, Latin, ancient Greek, Arabic, and German-English words came from all over the world and on their way accumulated (from the Latin *ad*, meaning "to" and *cumulus*, "heap, pile," which is also the name of a common cloud, the cumulus, or "heap" cloud) bits and bobs which help make them the unique words we know today.

Inside of invention—which we usually think of as a word meaning to create something completely brand new—is also a word from Latin, *inventus*, which comes from *invenio*, or, "I find." How can you both find something and create it??

But, as a matter of fact, lots of incredible things that we think of as inventions were found by accident, or when looking for something else.

Take, for example, penicillin, an antibiotic used to treat bacterial infections from the Greek *bakterion*, meaning "staff" or "cane." So-named because the first observed bacteria were hook-shaped, like canes). It was found by a scientist in London when he saw

that a mold growing on bacteria that had accidentally been left open to the air was actually preventing the bacteria's growth!

Other things invented by chance: potato chips (by a chef, frustrated with a picky eater); velcro (by an engineer, walking in the forest); Play-Doh (by a cleaner trying to get rid of coal marks). And so many more, including: Coca-Cola, microwaves, the Slinky, and even chocolate chip cookies!

So maybe another way to think about inventing something is to think of finding something... finding what you weren't looking for, finding what's now missing, finding the thing you don't yet have but need.

In this way, all that's required of being a good inventor—of words, cures, drinks, sweets, games, and more—is to be someone who pays attention, finds what is hidden, or notices the space that can only be filled by something new. ■

At a restaurant in New York in 1853, a customer complained that the fried potatoes on his plate were not only too soggy but also too thick.

After the meal was sent back to the chef several times with the same criticism, the chef—George Crum (hysterical name for a chef, no?)—was so enraged that he sliced the potatoes into paper thin slivers and fried them for the picky customer.

As you might have guessed, the customer loved them and so the first potato chip was born.

Meet:

KENAN MIROU

Kenan Mirou is originally from Damascus, Syria, and fled the country in 2012 with his family. As a Syrian, Mirou carries an urgency for helping his home country; he feels that sharing his aim with the global community is an important part of his identity. In 2018, Mirou gave a moving speech at the United Nations on the topic of the Syrian refugee crisis.

YOUTH activist

"In maintaining who we are, we make this country special by adding our characteristics, habits... and WAYS OF LIFE."

QUOTE FROM KENAN'S ESSAY "THIS IS US"

WHAT DID YOU FIND HELPFUL AS YOU MADE THE TRANSITION FROM SYRIA TO THE UNITED STATES?

We found such a warm and welcoming environment at our afterschool program at Mission High in San Francisco, California. We were able to gradually adjust to our new life.

DESCRIBE YOUR VISION FOR AN IMPROVED WORLD. WHAT WOULD YOU LIKE TO CHANGE?

I would love to see my home country Syria return to its former beauty. It is a fascinating place with the kindest hearts, and it deserves to have everyone help rebuild it.

WHAT ARE YOU CURRENTLY WORKING ON?

I am applying to medical school. I would like to become a pediatric orthopedic surgeon. I want to specialize in orthopedic surgery as it connects to a congenital deformity I have that has caused me to get over fourteen bone lengthening/correction surgeries done throughout my life, most of which were to fix past errors done by the last doctor.

IF THE WORLD ONLY KNEW

MIROU'S STORY IS INCLUDED IN THIS BOOK, PUBLISHED BY 826 VALENCIA, A WRITING PROGRAM SERVING YOUTH IN SAN FRANCISCO.

MIROU GIVING HIS SPEECH AT THE UNITED NATIONS IN 2018 IN GENEVA, SWITZERLAND.

the UNITED NATIONS building

AN INVITATION FOR A 100-YEAR BIRTHDAY PARTY

BY YULIA DROBOVA

interview with

OUR COVER ARTIST TAILI WU

Taili Wu is a Taiwanese stop-motion artist, illustrator, and ceramicist, currently based in New York. She loves creating work that sparks curiosity and imagination, often with a dash of humor.

Q: HOW DID YOU END UP WORKING IN CERAMICS?

A: In 2012, my boyfriend broke my favorite mug and we started looking for a replacement. We ended up taking a pottery class together and making our own. To this day, we still haven't made our favorite mug yet.

↳ *my childhood dream, rocking horse.*

← *toasted marshmallows, anyone?*

When I was little, goose farmers on scooters were every-where!

Q3 TELL US ABOUT A BOOK FROM CHILDHOOD THAT HAS INFLUENCED YOU.

A3 Akiko Hayashi's picture book *Miki's First Errand* is one of my favorites! It is a story about a little girl helping her mom to buy milk on her own. The picturesque images and details of the street and shops captured my eyes immediately. I enjoyed finding similarities from my childhood living in the countryside. I also love how brave and persistent little Miki is despite encountering so many obstacles.

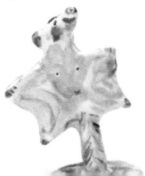

interview continued...

Q: DESCRIBE AN UNUSUAL OBJECT IN YOUR STUDIO.

A: On my desk, there is a wooden yellow bird whistle given by one of my mentors, Hoon, during my internship. He told me to use this whistle to call for help when I needed a hand because I was too shy to ask at the time. It has been sitting on my desk as a reminder to speak up.

Q: WHAT DO YOU TELL YOURSELF WHEN YOU ARE IN A DIFFICULT PART OF THE CREATIVE PROCESS?

A: Short: "加油! You are almost there!" (加油 pronounced as jiāyóu), literally meaning "add oil/fuel."

← *sculpting with blue foam.*

Q: WHAT'S NEXT ON YOUR ARTISTIC PLATE?

A: A short film, with my friend Anna Samo—a story about light & friendship.

Q: WHEN YOU WERE A KID, WHAT DID YOU WANT TO BE WHEN YOU GREW UP?

A: A maker of things!

Q: FAVORITE SNACK WHILE WORKING?

A: Piggy ear/kitten ear, a childhood snack from Taiwan.

"Q" is for QUOLL. (a marsupial

Q: ALBUM LISTENED TO RECENTLY?

A: Joe Hisaishi's *Ponyo on the Cliff by the Sea.*

X for XERUS

TYPOGRAPHICAL ART BY ADAM HIGTON.

MAKE THIS **INVENT @ FONT**

Try interpreting these themes using the alphabet to make your own font.

Aa Bb Cc Dd Ee Ff Gg Hh Ii
Jj Kk Ll Mm Nn Oo Pp Qq Rr
Ss Tt Uu Vv Ww Xx Yy Zz

Abstract ideas could include: shapes, dots / dashes, patterns.

Figurative ideas could involve animals or bugs.

What about plants or mushrooms?

What would it look like if a robot drew it?

ROBOT

A B C D E F G H
I J K L M N O

don't forget numbers —

1 2 3 4 5

How about if the letters were made of limp noodles?

noodle

Aa Bb Cc Dd

Try filling in the rest of this bird-themed alphabet:

FOR "H" REPEAT LEFT SIDE ON RIGHT

CAN YOU MAKE THE "G" BASED ON THE "C" ABOVE?

CAN YOU MAKE THE "J"

MIGHT THE "L" BE BASED ON "K"

draw, write, make

WRITE THIS SILLY short story

Fill in the blanks and write on the lines to invent your own tale about a silly contraption. What does it do? What does it fail to do?

I was in the lab again, determined to get over my previous failure, which was supposed to solve ____(world problem). Now I had a new vision to fix something for real.

What is the secret to my genius process? First of all, I gathered some _____(plural noun) and a rare _____(type of tool). It took ___(number) weeks and ___(number) days to finish.

* Explain how the new invention works:

* Explain more about your process:

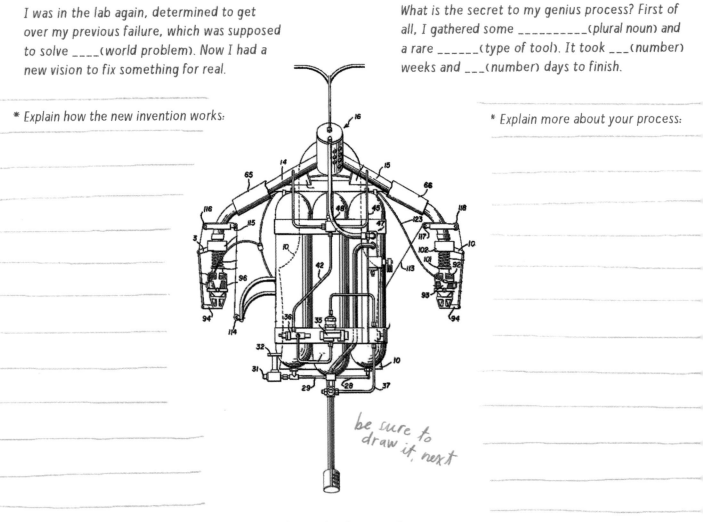

be sure to draw it, next

You won't believe what happened next. Instead of turning on, it _____(verb), and when I tried to shut it down completely, it made a noise just like a _____(sound).

* Surprise ending here.

Art supplies for
the ever-curious,
built by hand,
made to last.

MAJO

Sticker based art projects. Inspired by artists, created for kids.

DRAW THIS

INVENT → A NEW HAIRDO

Draw some new hairdos on these faces.
Maybe one of your designs will become all the rage?

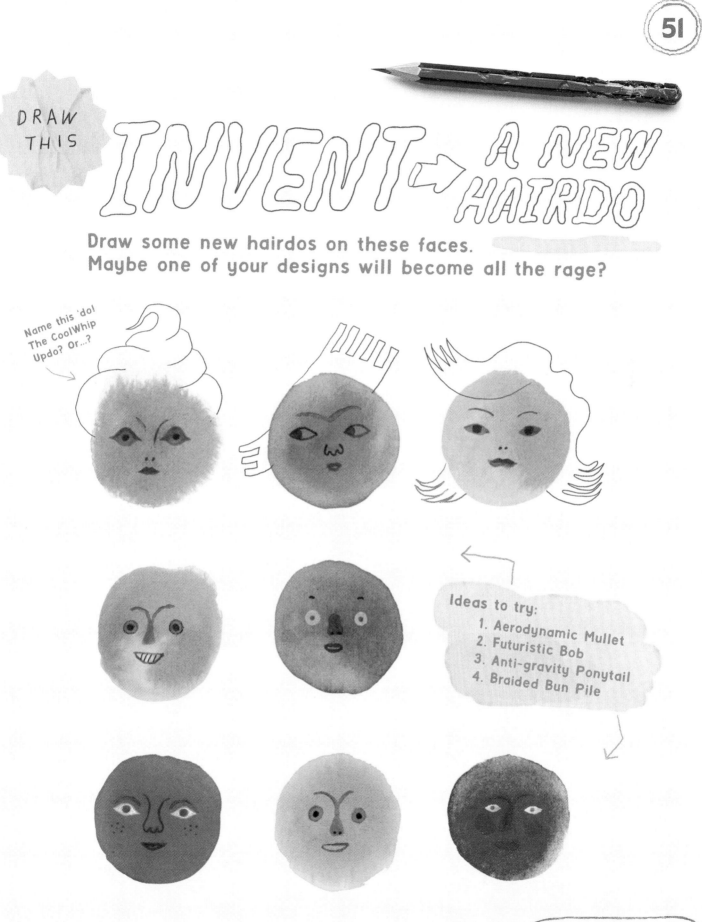

Name this 'do!
The CoolWhip
Updo? Or...?

Ideas to try:
1. Aerodynamic Mullet
2. Futuristic Bob
3. Anti-gravity Ponytail
4. Braided Bun Pile

draw, write, make

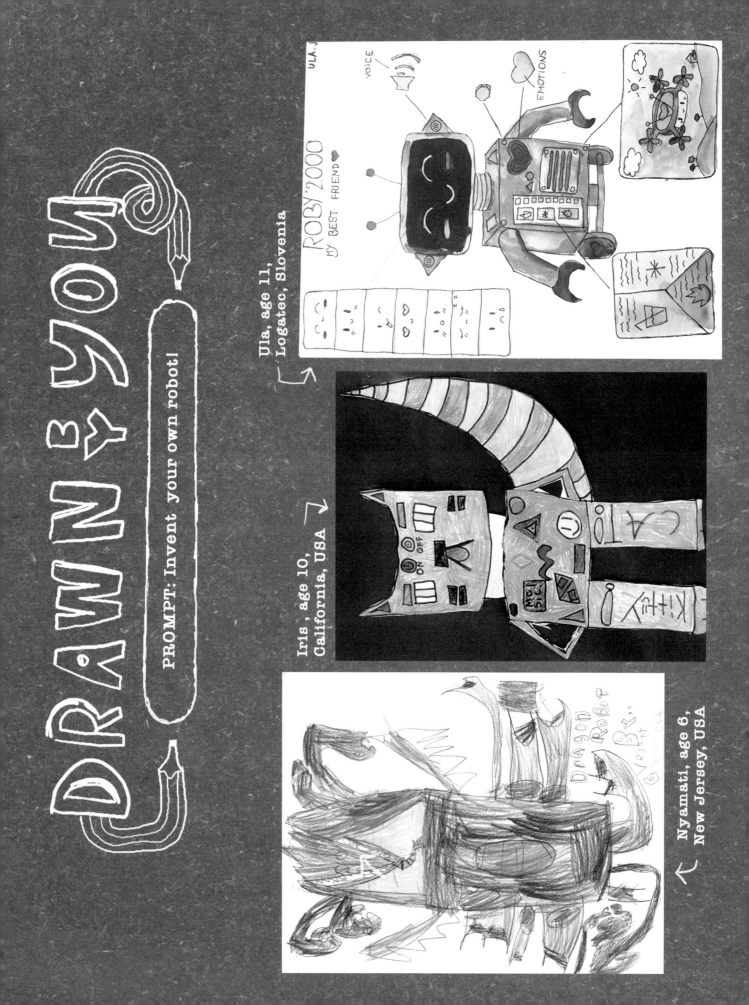

DRAWN BY YOU

PROMPT: Invent your own robot!

Ula, age 11,
Logatec, Slovenia.

Iris, age 10,
California, USA

Nyamati, age 6,
New Jersey, USA

Mia, age 8,
California, USA

Dylan, age 8, California, USA

Ian, age 7,
California, USA

Rien,
age 10,
Belgium

Follow our newsletter
to hear about upcoming
calls for youth artwork
submissions!

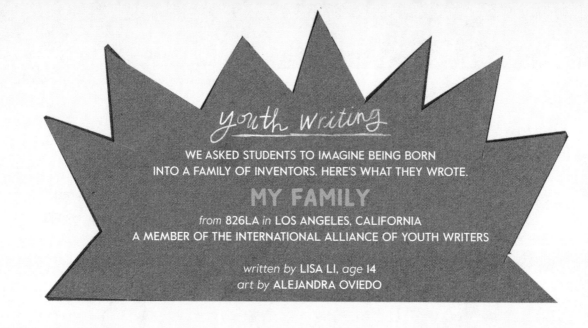

youth writing

WE ASKED STUDENTS TO IMAGINE BEING BORN
INTO A FAMILY OF INVENTORS. HERE'S WHAT THEY WROTE.

MY FAMILY

from 826LA in LOS ANGELES, CALIFORNIA
A MEMBER OF THE INTERNATIONAL ALLIANCE OF YOUTH WRITERS

written by LISA LI, age 14
art by ALEJANDRA OVIEDO

I WOKE UP TO A CLOUD OF SMOKE. I LOOKED AROUND MY ROOM. IT WAS FULL OF MY PARENTS' JUNK. I JUMPED OUT OF BED AND WALKED DOWN A LONG HALLWAY WHILE DODGING MY PARENTS' MESS. THERE'S BIG, SHINY TOOLS SCATTERED ALL OVER THE FLOOR. I HEARD LOUD, BOOMING NOISES COME FROM DOWN THE STAIRS. I CAREFULLY HOPPED DOWN THE WOODEN STAIRS TO ARRIVE AT THE DINING TABLE.

I WAS GREETED BY A BITTER SMELL. "MOM? DAD? WHAT ARE YOU TWO DOING?!" I YELLED. MY PARENTS WERE BOTH IN BRIGHT LAB COATS. THEY WERE ALSO COVERED IN DARK INK WHILE HOLDING A ROUND POTATO WITH SHARP SPIKES. MOM TURNED AND SAID, "OH! GOOD MORNING, WANT TO TRY SOME PANCAKES? A CAT MADE THEM!" I GLARED INTO THE KITCHEN TO SEE A FLUFFY GINGER CAT WITH A TALL CHEF HAT. IT WAS FLIPPING PANCAKES PERFECTLY. I QUICKLY TURNED TO MY MOM AND SHOUTED, "WHERE DID YOU GET A CAT FROM?! WHAT'S IT DOING HERE?"

DAD PROUDLY BRAGGED, "YOUR MOTHER AND I JUST INVENTED A CHEF HAT THAT PROGRAMS ANIMALS TO COOK!" I STARED AT HIM FOR A WHILE BEFORE SAYING, "YEAH I'M JUST GOING TO SCHOOL. I'M NOT HUNGRY". MOM SUDDENLY SCREECHED. "WAAAIT!! YOU'RE STILL A GROWING CHILD! YOU MUST EAT BREAKFAST." DAD HANDED ME A BROWN LUNCH BAG.

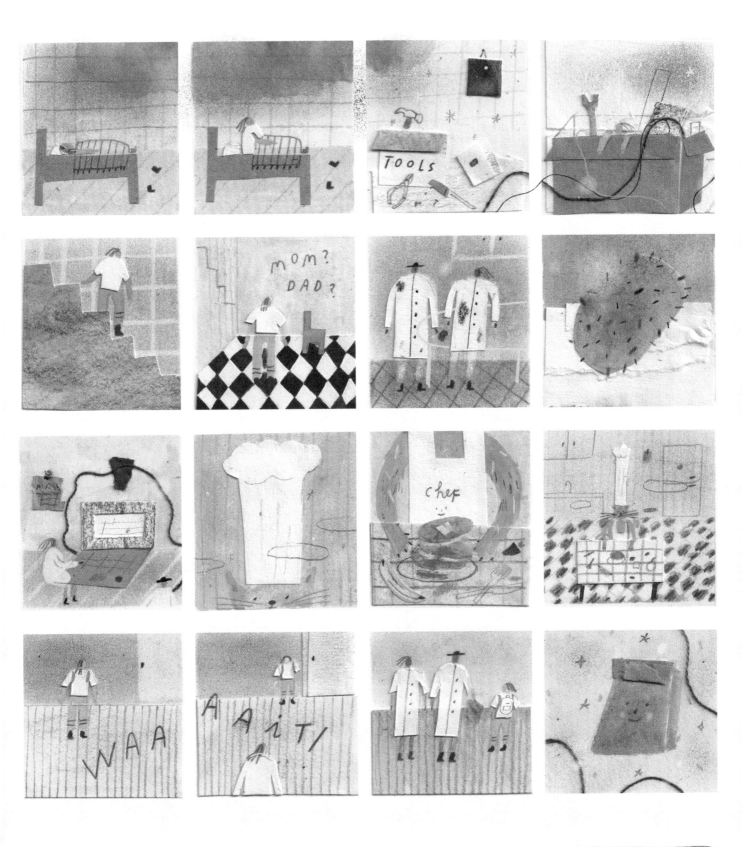

youth writing

WE ASKED STUDENTS TO IMAGINE BEING BORN
INTO A FAMILY OF INVENTORS. HERE'S WHAT THEY WROTE.

A CRAZY HOUSE, MY FAMILY, AND ME

from W*ORT *in* LUSTENAU, AUSTRIA
A MEMBER OF THE INTERNATIONAL ALLIANCE OF YOUTH WRITERS

written by CAROLINE OBERLEITNER, *age* 13
art by CHARLOTTE AGER

Mum scolds. But I don't care. Nobody is scolding me. Veronika is probably causing stress again. Veronika is my big sister and she's fifteen years old. But I am smarter. Even though I am only twelve years old and my room has been uninhabitable since yesterday's explosion. It really wasn't my fault that the automatic razor blew up. I wanted to give it to my dad for his birthday. But first things first: My family and I (that's mum, dad, Veronika, and grandma) live in the "House of a Thousand Ideas." We came up with this name ourselves.

Veronika and I are sisters, but we are also rivals. Who is smarter? That's the eternal question here. But since the explosion my flow of creativity has been interrupted. And since my room is uninhabitable, I am temporarily living in the spare room. Everything is so.... normal... in this room. I already miss my bed with the animated map of the stars on the ceiling. And "boom." Grandma enters the room with smoking hair.

I roll my eyes. Grandma's inventions always blow up. So annoying! Veronika also shuffles

into the room. She looks as if she had been sent down the chimney. I have to giggle. Grandma smiles, "The painting-re-drawing-machine maybe wasn't such a good idea."

"I could have told you years ago," Veronika hisses.

Now mum joins us. She looks even more upset. Behind her, dad struts into the room. He is wearing his research coat. He must have been working. I gather my concentration, as what comes next can be rather nerve-racking.

Just then, the whole Wonkystone family starts to argue. So it arrived: The big Friday discussion about whether grandma Erna should be allowed to continue her research. Mum and dad think she should retire. Enough is enough.

"That's enough! Get out! Immediately!"

That worked. The Wonkystones leave the room in a hurry. And I am alone again. This family of inventors can be rather exhausting, but also an incredible amount of fun. I couldn't do without them.

That was an insight into my family. And now I even have a new idea for an invention. So there was something good in all of this.

draw, write, make

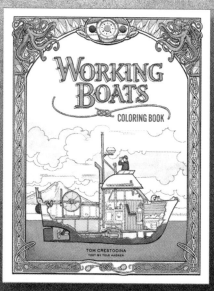

WORKING BOATS
COLORING BOOK

TOM CRESTODINA
TEXT BY TELE AADSEN

WORKING BOATS

Explore the fascinating
world of working boats
in these books that celebrate
the maritime community and
share in detail what it's like
to live and work aboard a
variety of boats.

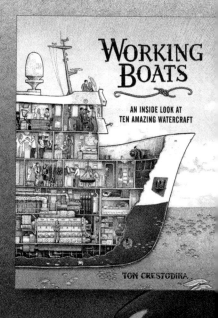

WORKING BOATS

AN INSIDE LOOK AT
TEN AMAZING WATERCRAFT

TOM CRESTODINA

little bigfoot
an imprint of sasquatch books
sasquatchbooks.com

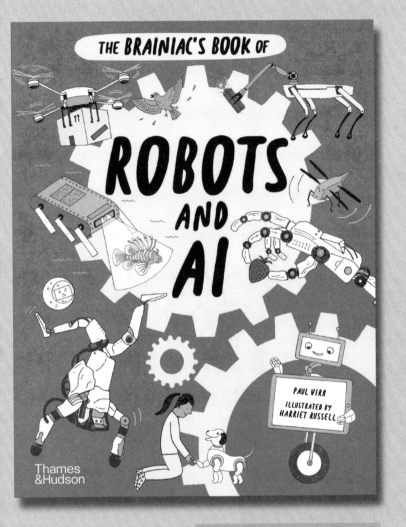
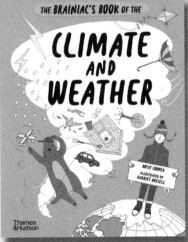

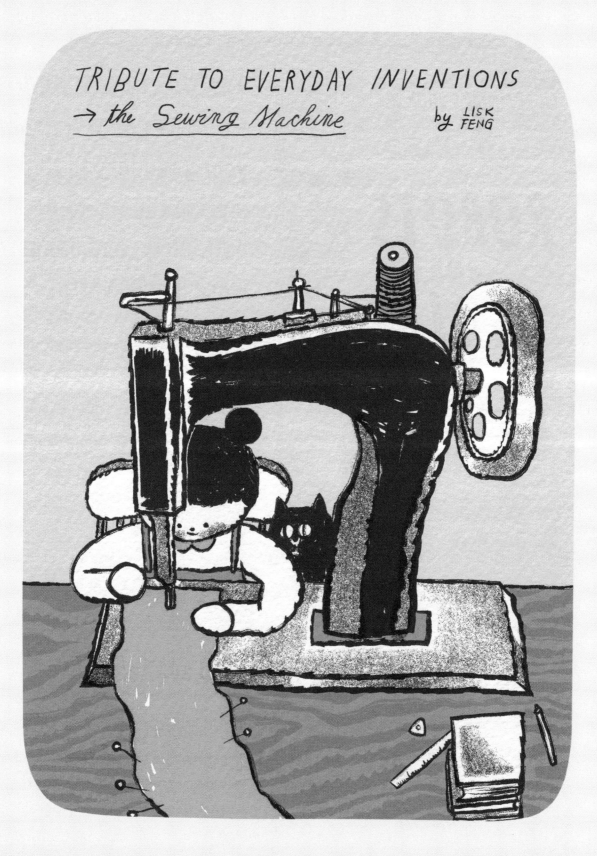

TYPOGRAPHICAL ART BY ADAM HIGTON.

ON OUR PLAYLIST:

Picked by CLAIRE ASTROW, our illustrious Editorial and Marketing Manager.

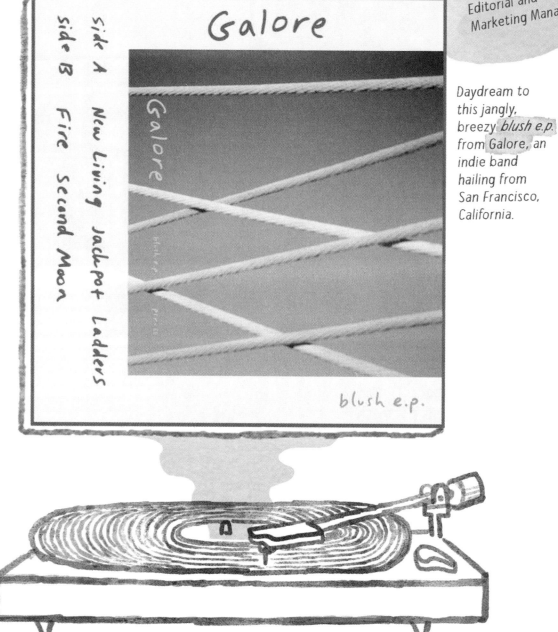

Galore

side A New Living Jackpot Ladders

side B Fire Second Moon

Galore

blush e.p.

Daydream to this jangly, breezy *blush e.p.* from Galore, an indie band hailing from San Francisco, California.

LISTEN TO OUR FULL PLAYLIST FOR THIS ISSUE ON SPOTIFY. USE THIS QR CODE TO DELVE INTO AN HOUR OF EAR-TINGLING TUNES... THE PERFECT BACKDROP TO JUMP INTO ONE OF THE DIY PROJECTS FROM CHAPTER 3.

ON OUR DESK:

BEROL COLOUR BROAD BLACK
I used these pens at school, great for big bold lines or night sky scenes.

Selected by one of our favorite artists to work with, ADAM HIGTON. Adam is an artist and musician based in York, UK. He make collages, carpets, cartoons, and songs.

HAY SCISSORS
These are nice scissors, light weight and comfortable. I bought my first pair many years ago and have never looked back since.

PRITT STICK
Best glue stick you can get, easy to stick small bits of paper without getting glue everywhere!

UNI PIN 0.8
I used to work with biro and then a 0.5 but found the lines were too scratchy, this is the perfect pen.

FAVORITE SNACK
Peanut butter on celery.

Look and listen

WE ASKED YOU TO TELL US ABOUT YOUR FAVORITE BIOGRAPHY

CONTEST

HOW TO BUILD A HUG

by:

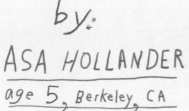

ASA HOLLANDER
age 5, Berkeley, CA

HOW TO BUILD A HUG: TEMPLE GRANDIN AND HER AMAZING SQUEEZE MACHINE
words by Amy Guglielmo and Jacqueline Tourville // art by Giselle Potter

I like that *How to Build a Hug* really showed Temple Grandin's life and how she changed over the years. Her first invention was a hug machine that made her feel calmer. Later she made a hug machine for cows. Someday I will make an invention where you pull a string and type the name of something you need and then a claw will put it on a conveyor belt.

ON OUR BOOKSHELF

A mysterious, wordless picture book about a strange tale that fell from the sky. Who invented this?

-words by
BRUCE HANDY
-art by
JULIE BENBASSAT

See more of Julie's art on page 28, in CREATURE FEATURE

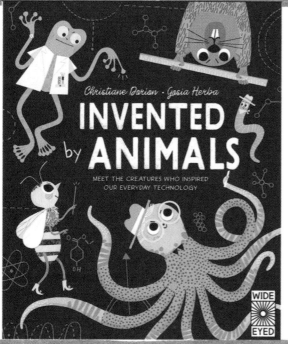

Meet the creatures who inspired human beings to invent the technology we use on a daily basis. It'll inspire you to take a closer look at the worlds of animals, amphibians, and insects.

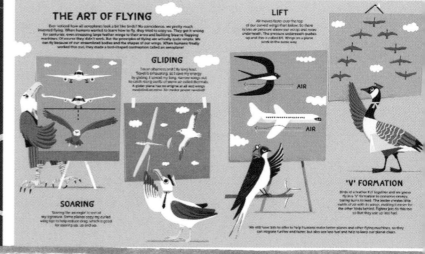

-words by
CHRISTIANE DORIAN
-art by
Gosia Herba

So, birds taught us how to fly, but what can we learn from SQUIDS?

-words by
JOHN CASSIDY & BRENDAN BOYLE

Now, you try! Start with these cleverly curated DIY projects. Nose-warmers, anyone?

future career? →

A fascinating angle on history!
-words by CHARLOTTE FOLTZ JONES
-art by JOHN O'BRIEN

what? cheese... an ACCIDENT?!

Follow a stone-age woolly mammoth as she jumps into stunningly detailed images about how even the most ordinary things function: from can openers to zippers.

stuff we've ALWAYS been wondering-

-by DAVID MACAULAY

now you know what a SPUR GEAR is... Look and listen

Deeper Dive!

...CONTINUED FROM PAGE 24
PROCESS INTERVIEW

Find more about how risograph printing works at:
www.risottostudio.com/pages/what-is-risograph-printing

...FIND A RISOPRINT CENTER IN A CITY NEAR YOU:

OAKLAND, CALIFORNIA
Floss Editions
www.flosseditions.com

PORTLAND, OREGON
Outlet
www.outletpdx.com

BROOKLYN, NEW YORK
Lucky Risograph
www.luckyrisograph.press

LOS ANGELES, CALIFORNIA
Tiny Splendor Press
www.tinysplendor.com

CHICAGO, ILLINOIS
Perfectly Acceptable
www.perfectly-acceptable.com

A FRINGE-GILLED AXOLOTL

THE STINGING IO MOTH CATERPILLAR

from page 29

MY STARS! A PANGOLIN?

CREATURE FEATURE, page 29

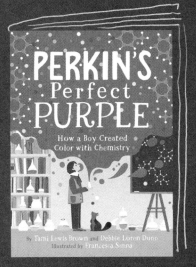

← learn more about this TEEN INVENTOR

-from page 30

...CONTINUED FROM PAGE 28
CREATURE FEATURE:
INVENTIVE SURVIVAL STRATEGIES

You'll want to look up more photos of these fascinating creatures! Here's a close up of an axolotl, stinging caterpillar, and a pangolin.

...CONTINUED FROM PAGE 30
ACCIDENTAL INVENTION

Want to learn more about William Henry Perkin, a young inventor? Check out *Perkin's Perfect Purple: How a Boy Created Color with Chemistry* by Tami Lewis Brown and Debbie Loren Dunn, illustrated by Francesca Sanna.

William Henry Perkin made other advances possible—including canned food and chemotherapy—but got his early start with the creation of synthetic purple.

...CONTINUED FROM PAGE 32
WE ASKED A POET WITH LAYLA FORREST-WHITE

Read this article that we gave our guest poet to read, about accidental discoveries:

"10 Inventions That Changed The World, But Were Made By Mistake"

Credit:
Prabhune, Akanksha. "10 Inventions That Changed The World, But Were Made By Mistake." Storypick, March 24, 2015.
www.storypick.com/inventions-made-by-mistake/

ANSWER KEY FROM WORD SLEUTH

on page 9

Look and listen

LET'S MAKE A BOOK!

Today.

Right now.

Go and find some paper.

I'll wait for you here.

READY?

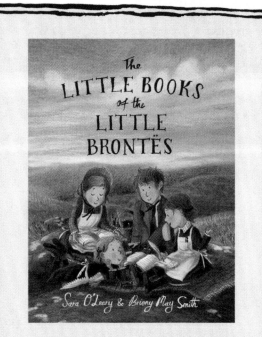

HOW TO MAKE YOUR OWN
LITTLE BOOK

There are a couple of ways you can make your own book, but my favorite is to take four pieces of paper and cut them in half. Then fold that little stack of pages in half. This will give you a book of thirty-two pages, which is the length of many picture books.

Next, find some construction paper, or something a little heavier than your pages. Fold it over your pages and trim to the right size for a cover. The Brontës used scraps of wallpaper for some of the books they made.

Now you can give your book a title. You can draw or paint a cover illustration. And you can say who the book is by — you!

The Brontës sewed their little books together with a needle and thread. You can do that, too, with some help from an adult. Or you can slip a rubber band around the fold or staple along the edge. If you use staples, you can cover them over with colored tape to make it look like a ribbon spine.

When you are done, you will have a very nice little book of your own, a little like the ones that the Brontës made, and a little like the one you see here! Now all you need is a story . . .

Share your little book with us
🐦 📷 @TundraBooks

This little book craft is featured in *The Little Books of the Little Brontës*, the inspiring true tale of young siblings who loved to invent stories and make books — and who grew up to be among English literature's finest writers.

tundra

A new picture book from

STEVE LIGHT

published by Candlewick Press

Itsy Bitsy sits at home, drinking tea, all alone . . .

Everyone knows the rhyme "The Itsy Bitsy Spider."
We know about the climb up the waterspout,
the washout, the return of the sun, and the
determined climb back up the spout—again.

But why did Itsy Bitsy make this famous journey?

Well, it all starts when a branch falls from a tree . . .

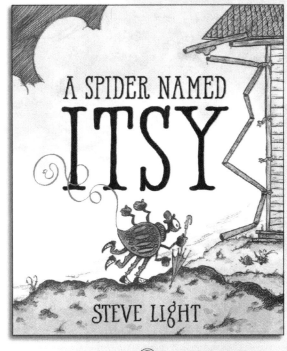

STEVE LIGHT is the creator of many books for young readers, including
Have You Seen My Dragon?, *Swap!*, and *Road Trip! A Whiskers Hollow
Adventure*. He lives in New York City with his wife and cat.

CANDLEWICK PRESS
www.candlewick.com

THE SKULL

A spooky folktale adaptation by

JON KLASSEN

This is an old story.

It is about a girl named Otilla who runs
away. It is also about a house in the
woods, and a skull who lives there, and a
secret the skull has, and the night that
Otilla finds out what that secret is.

JON KLASSEN is the creator of the best-selling
books *The Rock from the Sky* and *I Want My Hat Back*.
He lives in Los Angeles.

A NOTE FROM THE AUTHOR

I found this story in a library in Alaska. I thought about the story
every now and then for about a year. Finally, I thought, I should
probably read that story again. But when I sat down and read the
story again, I was surprised. It wasn't the story I remembered.
In the year in between, my brain had changed it without telling
me. This is a very interesting thing that our brains do to stories.
I like folktales because they are supposed to be changed by who
is telling them, and you never find them the
same way twice. I hope that you like my
brain's version.

CANDLEWICK PRESS
www.candlewick.com

THE YOUTH WRITING IN THIS ISSUE IS BY STUDENTS FROM

W*ORT in Lustenau, Austria
826LA in Los Angeles, California

TAKE A
TRIP AND
VISIT!

FIND A WRITING CENTER NEAR YOU ➡ YOUTHWRITING.ORG

In every issue of *Illustoria*, students from the The International Alliance of Youth Writing Centers contribute their own writing and art to add a range of voices to these pages. The International Alliance is joined in a common belief that young people need places where they can write and be heard, where they can have their voices polished, published, and amplified. There are nearly seventy centers worldwide. Learn more at www.youthwriting.org.